Step-by-Step, Practical Recipes Cupcakes: Contents

Teatime Treats

Small but perfectly formed, cupcakes are the ultimate teatime treat. With a multitude of flavours, take a bite of baking perfection.

Party Cupcakes

Want a cupcake that looks great and tastes even better? The cupcakes in this section will have you covered for celebrations throughout the year.

FLAME TREE has been creating family-friendly, classic and beginner recipes for our bestselling cookbooks for over 20 years now. Our mission is to offer you a wide range of expert-tested dishes, while providing clear images of the final dish so that you can match it to your own results. We hope you enjoy this super selection of recipes – there are plenty more to try! Titles in this series include:

Cupcakes • Slow Cooker • Curries
Soups & Starters • Baking & Breads
Cooking on a Budget • Winter Warmers
Party Cakes • Meat Eats • Party Food
Chocolate • Sweet Treats

www.flametreepublishing.com

Double Cherry Cupcakes

INGREDIENTS

Makes 12 large cupcakes or 18 fairy cakes

50 g/2 oz glacé
  cherries, washed,
  dried and chopped
125 g/4 oz self-raising flour
25 g/1 oz dried morello cherries
125 g/4 oz soft margarine
125 g/4 oz caster sugar
2 medium eggs
½ tsp almond extract

To decorate:

125 g/4 oz fondant
  icing sugar
pale pink liquid food colouring
40 g/1½ oz glacé cherries

1 Preheat the oven to 190°C/375°F/Gas Mark 5. Line a 12-hole muffin tray with deep paper cases, or two trays with 18 fairy-cake cases.

2 Dust the chopped glacé cherries lightly in a tablespoon of the flour, then mix with the morello cherries and set aside. Sift the rest of the flour into a bowl, then add the margarine, sugar, eggs and almond extract. Beat for about 2 minutes until smooth, then fold in the cherries.

3 Spoon the batter into the paper cases and bake for 15–20 minutes until well risen and springy in the centre. Turn out to cool on a wire rack.

4 To decorate the cupcakes, trim the tops level. Mix the icing sugar with 2–3 teaspoon warm water and a few drops of pink food colouring to make a thick consistency. Spoon the icing over each cupcake filling right up to the edge. Chop the cherries finely and sprinkle over the icing. Leave to set for 30 minutes. Keep for 3 days in an airtight container.

FOOD FACT

Glacé cherries come in a dark maroon natural colour and a brighter red colour, the latter usually being cheaper than the natural variety.

2

2

Ginger & Lemon Cupcakes

INGREDIENTS

Makes 18

8 tbsp golden syrup
125 g/4 oz block margarine
225 g/8 oz plain flour
2 tsp ground ginger
75 g/3 oz sultanas
50 g/2 oz soft dark
  brown sugar
200 ml/7 fl oz milk
1 tsp bicarbonate of soda
1 medium egg, beaten

To decorate:
125 g/4 oz golden icing sugar
1 tsp lemon juice
glacé ginger pieces

1   Preheat the oven to 180°C/350°F/Gas Mark 4. Line two shallow muffin trays with 18 paper cases.

2   Place the syrup and margarine in a heavy-based pan and melt together gently. Sift the flour and ginger into a bowl, then stir in the sultanas and sugar. Warm the milk and stir in the bicarbonate of soda.

3   Pour the syrup mixture, milk and beaten egg into the dry ingredients and beat until smooth. Pour the mixture into a jug.

4   Carefully spoon 2 tbsp of the mixture into each case (the mixture will be wet). Bake for about 30 minutes. Cool in the tins for 10 minutes, then turn out to cool on a wire rack.

5   To decorate, blend the icing sugar with the lemon juice and 1 tbsp warm water to make a thin glacé icing. Drizzle over the top of each cupcake, then top with glacé ginger pieces. Leave to set for 30 minutes. Keep in an airtight container for up to 5 days.

HELPFUL HINT
The best baking position for cupcakes is just above the centre of the oven and best results are achieved by baking only one tray at a time.

2

2

2

Crystallised Violet Cupcakes

INGREDIENTS

Makes 12

150 g/5 oz butter, softened

150 g/5 oz caster sugar

3 medium eggs, beaten

150 g/5 oz self-raising flour

½ tsp baking powder

1 lemon

To decorate:

12 fresh violets

1 egg white

caster sugar

125 g/4 oz fondant icing sugar

pale violet food colouring

1. Preheat the oven to 180°C/350°F/Gas Mark 4 and line a 12-hole muffin tray with deep paper cases.

2. Place the butter, sugar and eggs in a bowl. Sift in the flour and baking powder. Finely grate in the zest from the lemon.

3. Beat together for about 2 minutes with an electric hand mixer until pale and fluffy. Spoon into the paper cases and bake for 20–25 minutes until firm and golden. Cool on a wire rack.

4. To decorate the cupcakes, spread the violets on some nonstick baking parchment. Beat the egg white until frothy, then brush thinly over the violets. Dust with caster sugar and leave to dry out for 2 hours.

5. Beat the icing sugar with the colouring and enough water to give a thin coating consistency. Drizzle over the top of each cupcake quickly and top with a violet. Leave to set for 30 minutes. Store in an airtight container in a cool place. Keep for 2 days.

HELPFUL HINT

Before crystallising small flowers such as violets, clean the flowers with a clean brush, but do not wash them.

4

4

5

Chocolate Fudge Flake Cupcakes

INGREDIENTS

Makes 12 large cupcakes or 18 fairy cakes

125 g/4 oz self-raising flour
25 g/1 oz cocoa powder
125 g/4 oz soft margarine
125 g/4 oz soft light
  brown sugar
2 medium eggs, beaten
2 tbsp milk

To decorate:

25 g/1 oz butter
50 g/2 oz golden syrup
15 g/½ oz cocoa powder
125 g/4 oz golden icing sugar
25 g/1 oz cream cheese
40 g/1½ oz chocolate flake bars

1 Preheat the oven to 180°C/350°F/Gas Mark 4. Line a 12-hole muffin tray with deep paper cases, or one or two bun trays with 18 fairy-cake cases.

2 Sift the flour and cocoa powder into a large bowl, add the margarine, sugar, eggs and milk and whisk with an electric beater for about 2 minutes until smooth.

3 Divide the mixture between the paper cases and bake for about 20 minutes for the larger cupcakes and 15 minutes for the fairy cakes until a skewer inserted into the middle comes out clean. Turn out to cool on a wire rack.

4 To make the topping, melt the butter with the syrup and cocoa powder in a pan. Cool, then whisk in the icing sugar until the mixture has thickened, and beat in the cream cheese. Spread the frosting over the cupcakes. Chop the flake bar into small chunks, then place one chunk in the centre of each cupcake. Keep for 2 days in a cool place.

2

2

4

Black Forest Cupcakes

INGREDIENTS

Makes 12 large cupcakes or 24 small cupcakes

1 tbsp cocoa powder
2 tbsp boiling water
175 g/6 oz self-raising flour
1 tsp baking powder
125 g/4 oz soft tub margarine
175 g/6 oz soft dark brown sugar
2 medium eggs
3 tbsp milk

To decorate:

125 g/4 oz dark chocolate
4 tbsp seedless raspberry
  jam, warmed
150 ml/¼ pint double cream
1 tbsp kirsch (optional)
12 natural-coloured glacé cherries

1 Preheat the oven to 180°C/350°F/Gas Mark 4. Line a 12-hole muffin tray with large paper cases, or one or two bun trays with 24 small paper cases. Blend the cocoa powder with the boiling water and leave to cool.

2 Sift the flour and baking powder into a bowl and add the margarine, sugar, eggs, milk and the cocoa mixture. Whisk together for about 2 minutes until smooth, then spoon into the paper cases.

3 Bake for 15–20 minutes until springy to the touch. Cool in the tins for 5 minutes, then turn out onto a wire rack to cool.

4 To decorate the cupcakes, melt the chocolate and spread it out to cool on a clean plastic board. When it is almost set, pull a sharp knife through the chocolate to make curls. Refrigerate these until needed.

5 Brush the top of each cupcake with a little raspberry jam. Whisk the cream until it forms soft peaks, then fold in the kirsch, if using. Pipe or swirl the cream on top of each cupcake. Top with chocolate curls and whole glacé cherries for the large muffins or halved cherries for the smaller ones. Eat fresh or keep for 1 day in a cool place.

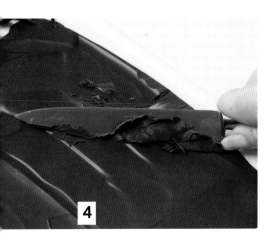

4

5

5

Mocha Cupcakes

INGREDIENTS

Makes 12

125 g/4 oz soft margarine
125 g/4 oz golden caster sugar
150 g/5 oz self-raising flour
2 tbsp cocoa powder
2 medium eggs
1 tbsp golden syrup
2 tbsp milk

To decorate:

225 g/8 oz golden icing sugar
125 g/4 oz unsalted
  butter, softened
2 tsp coffee extract
12 cape gooseberries, papery
  covering pulled back

1 Preheat the oven to 180°C/350°F/Gas Mark 4. Line a 12-hole muffin tray with deep paper cases.

2 Place the margarine and sugar in a large bowl, then sift in the flour and cocoa powder. In another bowl, beat the eggs with the syrup, then add to the cocoa mixture. Whisk everything together with the milk using an electric beater for 2 minutes, or by hand with a wooden spoon.

3 Divide the mixture between the cases, filling them three-quarters full. Bake for about 20 minutes until the centres are springy to the touch and a skewer inserted into the middle comes out clean. Turn out to cool on a wire rack.

4 Make the frosting by sifting the icing sugar into a bowl. Add the butter, coffee extract and 1 tbsp hot water. Beat until fluffy, then swirl onto each cupcake with a flat-bladed knife. Top each with a fresh cape goosberry. Keep for 2 days in a cool place.

HELPFUL HINT

Be careful when filling the paper cases with cake batter, as, if you spill the mixture onto the edges or outsides of the cases, it will cook and burn into dark brown marks that cannot be removed.

3

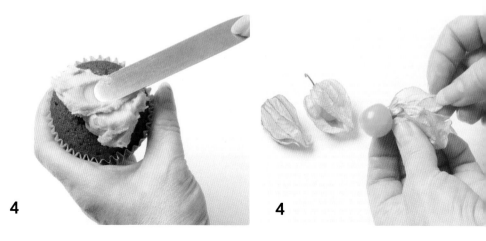

4

4

Mint Choc Chip Cupcakes

INGREDIENTS

Makes 12

125 g/4 oz soft margarine
125 g/4 oz golden caster sugar
2 medium eggs
175 g/6 oz self-raising flour
25 g/1 oz cocoa powder
1 tsp baking powder
75 g/3 oz dark chocolate chips
25 g/1 oz clear hard peppermint
  sweets, crushed into crumbs

To decorate:

50 g/2 oz unsalted butter
175 g/6 oz icing sugar
peppermint flavouring or extract
green food colouring
50 g/2 oz chocolate squares

1   Preheat the oven to 180°C/350°F/Gas Mark 4. Line a 12-hole muffin tray with deep paper cases.

2   Place the margarine, sugar and eggs in a bowl, then sift in the flour, cocoa powder and baking powder. Beat by hand or with an electric mixer until smooth. Then fold in the chocolate chips and the crushed mints.

3   Spoon the mixture into the paper cases and bake for 15–20 minutes until firm in the centre. Remove to a wire rack to cool.

4   Beat the butter and icing sugar together with 1 tbsp warm water, the peppermint extract and the food colouring. Place in a piping bag with a star nozzle and pipe swirls on top of each cupcake. Cut the chocolate into triangles and place one on top of each cake. Keep for 3–4 days in an airtight container in a cool place.

FOOD FACT

Flavouring extracts, such as the peppermint extract used here, are very concentrated and usually sold in liquid form in small bottles.

4

4

4

Chocolate & Toffee Cupcakes

INGREDIENTS

Makes 12–14

125 g/4 oz soft fudge
125 g/4 oz soft margarine
125 g/4 oz golden caster sugar
150 g/5 oz self-raising flour
2 tbsp cocoa powder
2 medium eggs
1 tbsp golden syrup

For the cream cheese frosting:

50 g/2 oz unsalted butter, softened at room temperature
300 g/11 oz icing sugar, sifted
flavouring of choice
125 g/4 oz full-fat cream cheese

1 Preheat the oven to 180°C/350°F/Gas Mark 4. Line one or two bun trays with 12–14 paper cases, depending on the depth of the holes. Cut one quarter of the fudge into slices for decoration. Chop the rest into small cubes. Set all the fudge aside.

2 Place the margarine and the sugar in a large bowl and then sift in the flour and cocoa powder. In another bowl, beat the eggs with the syrup, then add to the flour mixture. Whisk together with an electric beater for 2 minutes, or by hand with a wooden spoon until smooth. Gently fold in the fudge cubes.

3 Spoon the mixture into the cases, filling them three-quarters full. Bake for about 15 minutes until a skewer inserted into the centre comes out clean. Turn out to cool on a wire rack.

4 Make the cream cheese frosting. Beat the butter and icing sugar together until light and fluffy. Add flavourings of choice and beat again. Add the cream cheese and whisk until light and fluffy. Do not over-beat, however, as the mixture can become runny.

5 Swirl the cream cheese frosting over each cupcake, then finish by topping with a fudge slice. These cupcakes will keep for 3–4 days in a sealed container.

1

3

5

Gingerbread Cupcakes

INGREDIENTS

Makes 14–16

8 tbsp golden syrup
125 g/4 oz block margarine
225 g/8 oz plain flour
2 tsp ground ginger
75 g/3 oz sultanas
50 g/2 oz soft dark brown sugar
175 ml/6 fl oz milk
1 tsp bicarbonate of soda
1 medium egg, beaten
125 g/4 oz golden icing sugar,
  to decorate

1 Preheat the oven to 180°C/350°F/Gas Mark 4. Line one or two muffin trays with 14–16 deep paper cases, depending on the size of the holes.

2 Place the syrup and margarine in a heavy-based pan and melt together gently. Sift the flour and ginger into a bowl, then stir in the sultanas and sugar.

3 Warm the milk and stir in the bicarbonate of soda. Pour the syrup mixture, the milk and beaten egg into the dry ingredients and beat until smooth.

4 Spoon the mixture halfway up each case and bake for 25–30 minutes until risen and firm. Cool in the tins for 10 minutes, then turn out to cool on a wire rack.

5 To decorate the cupcakes, blend the icing sugar with 1 tbsp warm water to make a thin glacé icing. Place in a paper icing bag and snip away the tip. Drizzle over the top of each cupcake in a lacy pattern. Keep in an airtight container for up to 5 days.

FOOD FACT

Icing sugar is usally sold plain and white, but can also be bought as an unrefined golden (or 'natural' variety), as needed for this recipe.

2

2

4

Honey Spice Cupcakes

INGREDIENTS

Makes 12–14

1 tsp instant coffee granules

6 tbsp hot water

175 g/6 oz plain flour

1 tsp baking powder

½ tsp bicarbonate of soda

½ tsp ground cinnamon

½ tsp ground ginger

pinch ground cloves

2 medium eggs

125 g/4 oz golden
　caster sugar

175 g/6 oz honey

5 tbsp vegetable oil

50 g/2 oz walnuts,
　finely chopped

125 g/4 oz golden icing
　sugar, to decorate

1 Preheat the oven to 160°C/325°F/Gas Mark 3. Line one or two muffin trays with 12–14 deep paper cases, depending on the depth of the holes. Dissolve the coffee in the water and leave aside to cool.

2 Sift the flour with the baking powder, bicarbonate of soda and spices. In another bowl, beat the eggs with the sugar and honey until smooth and light, then gradually beat in the oil until blended. Stir this into the flour mixture along with the coffee and walnuts. Beat until smooth.

3 Carefully spoon the mixture into the paper cases. Fill each halfway up. Be careful not to overfill them, as the mixture will rise up. Bake for 25–30 minutes until they are risen, firm and golden. Leave in the tins for 5 minutes, then turn out onto a wire rack to cool.

4 To decorate, blend the icing sugar with 1 tbsp warm water to make a thin glacé icing. Place in a paper icing bag and snip away the tip. Pipe large daisies round the sides of each cupcake and leave to set for 30 minutes. Keep in an airtight container for up to 5 days.

1

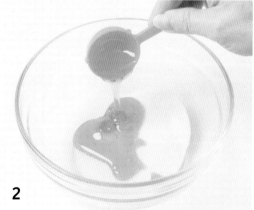

2

3

Scandinavian Apple Cupcakes

INGREDIENTS

Makes 12–14

125 g/4 oz self-raising flour
½ tsp ground cinnamon
125 g/4 oz caster sugar
125 g/4 oz soft margarine
2 medium eggs, beaten
1 tsp vanilla extract

To decorate:

150 g/5 oz unsalted butter,
  softened at room temperature
225 g/8 oz icing sugar, sifted
2 tbsp hot milk or water
1 tsp vanilla extract
600 g/1 lb 5 oz ready-to-roll
  sugarpaste
red, green and brown paste
  food colourings

1 Preheat the oven to 180°C/350°F/Gas Mark 4. Line two 12-hole bun trays with red paper or foil cases.

2 Sift the flour and cinnamon into a bowl and stir together with the caster sugar. Add the margarine and eggs and beat together with the vanilla extract for about 2 minutes until smooth.

3 Spoon into the cases and bake for 15–20 minutes until golden and firm to the touch. Turn out to cool on a wire rack. When cool, trim the tops flat if they have peaked slightly.

4 To make the buttercream, beat the butter until light and fluffy, then beat in the sifted icing sugar and hot milk or water in two batches. Add the vanilla extract. Lightly coat the top of each cupcake with a little buttercream.

5 Dust a clean flat surface with icing sugar. Colour one quarter of the sugarpaste red, one quarter green and a few scraps brown, leaving the rest white. Roll out the white sugarpaste and stamp out circles 6 cm/2½ inches wide. Place on top of each cupcake and smooth level. Mould the green and red sugarpaste into round apple shapes and place on top of the white icing. Decorate with small green leaves and brown stalks. Keep for 3 days in an airtight container in a cool place.

5

5

5

Ruffled Cupcakes

INGREDIENTS

Makes 12

125 g/4 oz self-raising flour
125 g/4 oz caster sugar
125 g/4 oz soft margarine
2 medium eggs, beaten
1 tsp lemon juice
1 tbsp milk

To decorate:

150 g/5 oz unsalted butter,
  softened at room temperature
225 g/8 oz icing sugar, sifted
2 tbsp hot milk or water
1 tsp vanilla extract
450 g/1 lb ready-to-roll sugarpaste

1 Preheat the oven to 180°C/350°F/Gas Mark 4. Line a 12-hole bun tray with paper cases or silicone moulds.

2 Sift the flour into a bowl and stir together with the caster sugar. Add the margarine and eggs and beat together with the lemon juice and milk for about 2 minutes until smooth.

3 Spoon into the cases and bake for 15–20 minutes until golden and firm to the touch. Turn out on a wire rack. When cool, trim the tops flat if they have formed peaks. Make the buttercream. Beat the butter until light and fluffy, then beat in the sifted icing sugar and hot milk or water in two batches. Add the vanilla extract. Spread buttercream over the flat surfaces.

4 Dust a clean flat surface with icing sugar. Roll out the sugarpaste and stamp out a fluted circle 6 cm/2½ inches wide. Cut a small plain 3 cm/1 inch wide circle out of the centre and discard. Take a cocktail stick and roll this back and forth in the sugarpaste circle until it begins to frill up. Take the frilled circle and place on the buttercream, fluting up the edges. Make another fluted circle and cut a break in the ring, then coil this round inside the first layer. Roll a pea-sized ball and place this in the centre. Serve dusted with icing sugar. Keep for 3 days in a cool place in an airtight container.

3

3

4

Mini Valentine Heart Cupcakes

INGREDIENTS

Makes 24

125 g/4 oz soft margarine
125 g/4 oz caster sugar
2 medium eggs, beaten
1 tsp vanilla extract
1 tbsp milk
125 g/4 oz self-raising flour

To decorate:

pink and red paste food colouring
225 g/8 oz ready-to-roll sugarpaste
50 g/2 oz ready-made royal icing
50 g/2 oz unsalted butter, softened at
  room temperature
300 g/11 oz icing sugar, sifted
flavouring of choice
125 g/4 oz full-fat cream cheese

1. Preheat the oven to 180°C/350°F/Gas Mark 4 and line a 24-hole mini-muffin tray with mini paper cases.

2. Place the margarine, sugar, eggs, vanilla extract and milk in a bowl, then sift in the flour. Beat together for about 2 minutes with an electric hand mixer until pale and fluffy.

3. Spoon into the paper cases and bake for 14–18 minutes until firm and golden. Cool on a wire rack.

4. To decorate, dust a clean flat surface with icing sugar. Colour one third of the sugarpaste pink and one third red. Leave the rest white. Roll out the sugarpaste thinly and, using a cutter, cut out pink, red and white heart shapes. Press onto a cocktail stick and then secure with a little royal icing. Leave to dry flat and harden for 2 hours on greaseproof paper.

5. Make the cream cheese frosting. Beat the butter and icing sugar together until light and fluffy. Add flavourings of choice and beat again. Add the cream cheese and whisk until light and fluffy. Do not over-beat, however, as the mixture can become runny. Colour the cream cheese frosting pale pink and place in a piping bag fitted with a star nozzle.

6. Pipe a swirl on top of each cupcake and decorate each one with a heart. Keep in a cool place for up to 2 days. Remember to remove the cocktail sticks before eating the cupcakes.

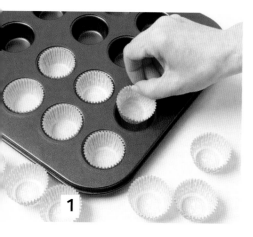

1

3

4

Mother's Day Rose Cupcakes

INGREDIENTS

Makes 12

125 g/4 oz caster sugar
125 g/4 oz soft tub margarine
2 medium eggs
125 g/4 oz self-raising flour
1 tsp baking powder
1 tsp rosewater

To decorate:

50 g/2 oz ready-to-roll sugarpaste
pink paste food colouring
350 g/12 oz fondant icing sugar

HELPFUL HINT

Paste food colourings are best for working with sugarpaste and a little goes a very long way. As these are very conentrated, use a cocktail stick to add dots of paste gradually, until you are sure of the colour, and knead in until even.

1 Preheat the oven to 190°C/375°F/Gas Mark 5. Line a 12-hole bun tray with paper cases.

2 Place all the cupcake ingredients in a large bowl and beat with an electric mixer for about 2 minutes until smooth. Fill the paper cases halfway up with the mixture. Bake for about 15 minutes until firm, risen and golden. Remove to a wire rack to cool.

3 To decorate the cupcakes, first line an egg box with foil and set aside. Colour the sugarpaste icing with pink paste food colouring. Make a small cone shape, then roll a pea-sized piece of sugarpaste into a ball. Flatten out the ball into a petal shape and wrap this round the cone shape. Continue adding more petals to make a rose, then trim the thick base, place in the egg box and leave to dry out for 2 hours.

4 Blend the fondant icing sugar with a little water to make a thick icing of spreading consistency, then colour this pale pink. Smooth over the top of each cupcake and decorate with the roses immediately. Leave to set for 1 hour. These cupcakes will keep for 1 day in an airtight container.

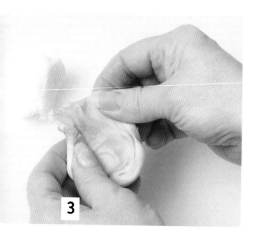

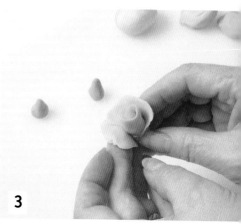

Father's Day Cupcakes

INGREDIENTS

Makes 14

125 g/4 oz self-raising flour
125 g/4 oz caster sugar
125 g/4 oz soft margarine
2 medium eggs, beaten
1 tsp vanilla extract

To decorate:

150 g/5 oz unsalted butter,
  softened at room temperature
225 g/8 oz icing sugar, sifted
2 tbsp hot milk or water
1 tsp vanilla extract
blue, yellow and orange paste
  food colouring
225 g/8 oz ready-to-roll sugarpaste
50 g/2 oz royal icing sugar
edible silver balls

1   Preheat the oven to 180°C/350°F/Gas Mark 4. Line two 12-hole bun trays with 14 paper fairy-cake cases or silicone moulds.

2   Sift the flour into a bowl and stir together with the caster sugar. Add the margarine, eggs and vanilla extract and beat together for about 2 minutes until smooth.

3   Spoon into the cases and bake for 15–20 minutes until golden and firm to the touch. Turn out on a wire rack. When cool, trim the tops flat if they have peaked slightly.

4   Make the buttercream. Beat the butter until light and fluffy, then beat in the sifted icing sugar and hot milk or water in two batches. Add the vanilla extract. Colour half the buttercream yellow and the other half orange and swirl over the top of each cupcake. Dust a clean flat surface with icing sugar. Colour the sugarpaste light blue and roll out thinly. Stamp out large stars 4 cm/1½ inches wide and place these on the buttercream.

5   Make up the royal icing mix and place in a paper piping bag with the end snipped away and pipe 'Dad' or names on the stars. Decorate with the edible silver balls. These cupcakes will keep for 3 days in an airtight container.

4

4

4

Pink Baby Bow Cupcakes

INGREDIENTS

Makes 12

125 g/4 oz self-raising flour
125 g/4 oz caster sugar
125 g/4 oz soft margarine
2 medium eggs, beaten
1 tsp vanilla extract
pink paste food colouring

To decorate:

150 g/5 oz unsalted butter,
    softened at room temperature
225 g/8 oz icing sugar, sifted
2 tbsp hot milk or water
1 tsp vanilla extract
 pink paste food colouring
225 g/8 oz ready-to-roll sugarpaste

1 Preheat the oven to 180°C/350°F/Gas Mark 4. Line a 12-hole muffin tray with deep paper cases or silicone moulds.

2 Sift the flour into a bowl and stir together with the caster sugar. Add the margarine, eggs and vanilla extract and beat together with a little pink paste food colouring to give a delicate pink. Beat for about 2 minutes until smooth.

3 Spoon into the cases and bake for 20 minutes, or until golden and firm to the touch. Turn out on a wire rack. When cool, trim the tops flat if they have peaked slightly.

4 Make the buttercream. Beat the butter until light and fluffy, then beat in the sifted icing sugar and hot milk or water in two batches. Add the vanilla extract. Colour the buttercream pale pink, then colour the sugarpaste pink to match the buttercream. Dust a clean flat surface with icing sugar. Roll out the sugarpaste thinly and cut out long narrow strips 1½ cm/½ inch wide. Roll small squares of nonstick baking parchment into narrow tubes and fold the pink icing over these to form loops. Make 24 loops, two for each cupcake, and leave to dry out and firm up for 2 hours. Cut strips to form the ribbon ends of each bow and keep aside on nonstick baking parchment.

5 To finish off the cupcakes, spread the top of each one with pink buttercream, carefully remove the loops from the paper and position the bows in the icing. Place the ribbon pieces onto the cupcakes to finish. These cupcakes will keep for 3 days in a cool place in an airtight container.

3

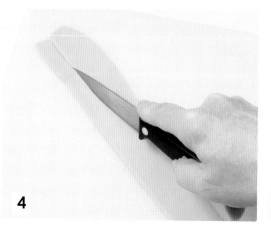

4

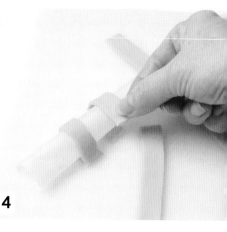

4

Quilted Cupcakes

INGREDIENTS

Makes 12–14

125 g/4 oz self-raising flour
125 g/4 oz caster sugar
125 g/4 oz soft margarine
2 medium eggs, beaten
1 tsp lemon juice

To decorate:

150 g/5 oz unsalted butter,
  softened at room temperature
225 g/8 oz icing sugar, sifted
2 tbsp hot milk or water
1 tsp vanilla extract
450 g/1 lb ready-to-roll sugarpaste
edible gold or silver balls

1 Preheat the oven to 180°C/350°F/Gas Mark 4. Line two 12-hole bun trays with 12–14 foil cases, depending on the depth of the holes.

2 Sift the flour into a bowl and stir together with the caster sugar. Add the margarine and eggs and beat together with the lemon juice for about 2 minutes until smooth.

3 Spoon into the cases and bake for 15–20 minutes until golden and firm to the touch. Turn out on a wire rack. When cool, trim the tops flat if they have peaked slightly.

4 Make the buttercream. Beat the butter until light and fluffy, then beat in the sifted icing sugar and hot milk or water in two batches. Add the vanilla extract. Lightly coat the top of each cupcake with a little buttercream.

5 Dust a clean flat surface with icing sugar. Roll out the sugarpaste and stamp out circles 6 cm/2½ inches wide. Place these on the buttercream to cover the top of each cupcake. Take a palette knife and press lines into the icing, then mark across in the opposite direction to make small squares. Place an edible gold or silver ball into the corner of each square. Keep for 3 days in an airtight container in a cool place.

4

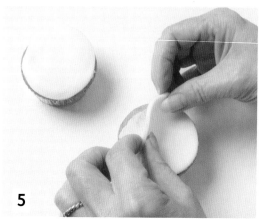

5

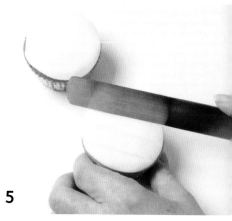

5

Hearts & Flowers Cupcakes

INGREDIENTS

Makes 12

150 g/5 oz butter, softened
150 g/5 oz caster sugar
175 g/6 oz self-raising flour
3 medium eggs, beaten
1 tsp lemon juice
1 tbsp milk

To decorate:

350 g/12 oz sugarpaste icing
paste food colourings
50 g/2 oz unsalted butter, softened at
  room temperature
300 g/11 oz icing sugar, sifted
flavouring of choice
125 g/4 oz full-fat cream cheese

1 Preheat the oven to 180°C/350°F/Gas Mark 4. Line a 12-hole muffin tray with deep paper cases.

2 Place the butter and sugar in a bowl, then sift in the flour. Add the beaten eggs to the bowl with the lemon juice and milk and beat until smooth. Spoon into the cases, filling them three-quarters full.

3 Bake for about 18 minutes until firm to the touch in the centre. Turn out to cool on a wire rack.

4 To decorate, colour the sugarpaste icing in batches in any colours you like. Dust a clean flat surface with icing sugar. Roll out the sugarpaste thinly and stamp out daisies using a flower stamp, then roll out some more sugarpaste thinly and cut out small heart shapes. Leave the sugarpaste shapes to dry out for 30 minutes until firm enough to handle.

5 Make the cream cheese frosting. Beat the butter and icing sugar together until light and fluffy. Add flavourings of choice and beat again. Add the cream cheese and whisk until light and fluffy. Do not over-beat, however, as the mixture can become runny. Place the frosting in a piping bag fitted with a star nozzle. Pipe swirls onto each cupcake. Press the flowers and hearts onto the frosting. Keep in an airtight container in a cool place for 3 days.

2

4

5

Silver Wedding Celebration Cupcakes

INGREDIENTS

Makes 24

150 g/5 oz butter, softened
150 g/5 oz caster sugar
150 g/5 oz self-raising flour
25 g/1 oz ground almonds
3 medium eggs, beaten
1 tsp almond extract
2 tbsp milk

To decorate:

350 g/12 oz sugarpaste icing
edible silver dusting powder
450 g/1 lb fondant icing sugar
24 small silver ribbon bows

HELPFUL HINT

Store cupcakes with sugarpaste decorations in a cool place, but not in the refrigerator. The moisture in a refrigerator will be absorbed by the sugarpaste and make this icing go limp and soggy.

1 Preheat the oven to 180°C/350°F/Gas Mark 4. Line two 12-bun trays with silver foil cases.

2 Place the butter and sugar in a bowl, then sift in the flour and stir in the almonds. Add the beaten eggs to the bowl along with the almond extract and milk and beat until smooth. Spoon into the cases, filling them three-quarters full.

3 Bake for about 18 minutes until firm to the touch in the centre. Turn out onto a wire rack. Once cool, trim the tops of the cupcakes if they have peaked.

4 To decorate the cupcakes, first line an egg box with foil. Roll the sugarpaste into pea-sized balls and mould each one into a petal shape. Mould a cone shape and wrap a petal completely round this. Take another petal and wrap round the first, overlapping. Continue wrapping 4–5 petals round until a rose has formed. Pull the thick base away, flute out the petals and place in the egg box. Repeat until you have 24 roses. Leave them to dry out for 2–4 hours. When they are firm, brush edible silver dust lightly over each rose with a clean paintbrush.

5 Make up the fondant icing sugar with water, according to the packet instructions, to a thick icing of a spreading consistency. Spread over the top of each cupcake. Work quickly, as this icing will set. Press a rose into the icing and place a thin silver bow on each cupcake. Leave to set for 30 minutes. Keep in a cool place for 2 days. Remove the bows before eating.

4

4

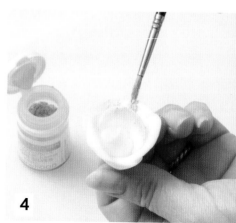

4

White Chocolate Christmas Cupcakes

INGREDIENTS

Makes 12–16

150 g/5 oz butter, softened
150 g/5 oz caster sugar
150 g/5 oz self-raising flour
3 medium eggs, beaten
1 tsp vanilla extract
1 tbsp milk
75 g/3 oz white chocolate,
  finely grated

To decorate:

150 g/5 oz unsalted butter,
  softened at room temperature
225 g/8 oz icing sugar, sifted
2 tbsp hot milk or water
1 tsp vanilla extract
250 g/9 oz white chocolate, chopped
16 holly leaves, cleaned and dried
icing sugar, for dusting

1 Preheat the oven to 180°C/350°F/Gas Mark 4. Line one or two 12-hole bun trays with 12–16 foil cases, depending on the depth of the holes.

2 Place the butter and sugar in a bowl, then sift in the flour. Add the eggs to the bowl with the vanilla extract and milk and beat until smooth. Fold in the grated white chocolate, then spoon into the cases, filling them three-quarters full. Bake for about 18 minutes until firm to the touch in the centre. Turn out to cool on a wire rack.

3 Make the buttercream. Beat the butter until light and fluffy, then beat in the sifted icing sugar and hot milk or water in two batches. Add the vanilla extract. Reserve.

4 Melt the white chocolate in a heatproof bowl standing over a pan of barely simmering water. Use one third of the melted chocolate to paint the underside of the holly leaves and leave to set for 30 minutes in the refrigerator. Spread one third of the chocolate out onto a clean plastic board. When almost set, make into curls by pulling a sharp knife through the chocolate at an angle until the chocolate curls away from the knife. Stir the remaining cooled chocolate into the buttercream and chill for 15 minutes.

5 Swirl each cupcake with buttercream, then press on the white chocolate curls. Peel the holly leaves away from the chocolate and carefully place on top of the cupcakes. Dust with icing sugar before serving. Keep for 2 days in a cool place.

4

4

4

Giftwrapped Presents Cupcakes

INGREDIENTS

Makes 12–14

125 g/4 oz butter
125 g/4 oz soft dark muscovado sugar
2 medium eggs, beaten
225 g/8 oz self-raising flour
1 tsp ground mixed spice
finely grated zest and 1 tbsp juice
   from 1 orange
1 tbsp black treacle
350 g/12 oz mixed dried fruit

To decorate:

3 tbsp sieved apricot glaze
icing sugar, for dusting
600 g/1 lb 5 oz ready-to-roll
   sugarpaste
red, blue, green and yellow paste
   food colourings

1 Preheat the oven to 180°C/350°F/Gas Mark 4. Line 1 or 2 12-hole muffin trays with 12–14 deep paper cases, depending on the depth of the holes.

2 Beat the butter and sugar together until light and fluffy, then beat in the eggs a little at a time, adding 1 tsp flour with each addition. Sift in the remaining flour and spice, add the orange zest and juice, treacle and dried fruit to the bowl and fold together until the mixture is blended.

3 Spoon into the cases and bake for about 30 minutes until firm in the centre and a skewer comes out clean. Leave to cool in the tins for 15 minutes, then turn out to cool on a wire rack. Store undecorated in an airtight container for up to 4 weeks, or freeze until needed.

4 To decorate, trim the top of each cupcake level if they have peaked, then brush with apricot glaze. Dust a clean flat surface with icing sugar. Colour the sugarpaste in batches and roll out thinly. Cut out circles 6 cm/2½ inches wide. Place a disc on top of each cupcake and press level. Mould coloured scraps into long thin sausages and roll these out thinly. Place a contrasting colour across each cupcake and arrange into bows and loops. Leave to dry for 24 hours if possible. Keep for 4 days in an airtight container.

4

4

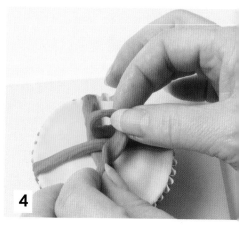

4

Crystallised Rosemary & Cranberry Cupcakes

INGREDIENTS

Makes 12

125 g/4 oz self-raising flour
125 g/4 oz butter, softened
125 g/4 oz golden caster sugar
2 medium eggs, beaten
zest of ½ orange, finely grated

To decorate:

1 egg white
12 small rosemary sprigs
125 g/4 oz fresh red cranberries
caster sugar, for dusting
3 tbsp apricot glaze, sieved
350 g/12 oz ready-to-roll sugarpaste

1 Preheat the oven to 180°C/350°F/Gas Mark 4. Line a 12-hole bun tray with foil fairy cake cases.

2 Sift the flour into a bowl and add the butter, sugar, eggs and orange zest. Beat for about 2 minutes until smooth, then spoon into the paper cases.

3 Bake in the centre of the oven for about 14 minutes until well risen and springy in the centre. Transfer to a wire rack to cool.

4 To decorate, place a sheet of nonstick baking parchment on a flat surface. Beat the egg white until frothy, then brush thinly over the rosemary and cranberries and place them on the nonstick baking parchment. Dust with caster sugar and leave to dry out for 2–4 hours until crisp.

5 Brush the top of each fairy cake with a little apricot glaze. Roll out the sugarpaste on a clean flat surface dusted with icing sugar and cut out 12 circles 6 cm/2½ inches wide. Place a disc on top of each and press level. Decorate each one with sparkly rosemary sprigs and cranberries. Keep for 3 days in an airtight container in a cool place.

HELPFUL HINT

To carry cupcakes to a special event, you will need to use a large flat plastic lidded box. These are ideal and you will find the best boxes are those that stack into each other for ease of carrying.

4

4

5

Glittery Outer Space Cupcakes

INGREDIENTS

Makes 18–20

125 g/4 oz soft margarine
125 g/4 oz caster sugar
125 g/4 oz self-raising flour
2 medium eggs
1 tsp vanilla extract
1 tbsp milk

To decorate:

125 g/4 oz ready-to-roll sugarpaste
edible coloured or glitter dust
50 g/2 oz unsalted butter, softened at
 room temperature
300 g/11 oz icing sugar, sifted
flavouring of choice
125 g/4 oz full-fat cream cheese
edible metallic coloured balls

1 Preheat the oven to 180°C/350°F/Gas Mark 4. Line a mini-muffin tray with 18–20 mini paper cases or silicone moulds, depending on the depth of the holes.

2 Place the margarine and sugar in a bowl, then sift in the flour. In another bowl, beat the eggs with the vanilla extract and milk, then add to the flour mixture. Beat until smooth, then spoon into the cases, filling them halfway up.

3 Bake for about 12–14 minutes until firm to the touch in the centre. Turn out to cool on a wire rack.

4 Place a large piece of nonstick baking parchment on a flat surface. Roll the sugarpaste into pea-sized balls on the paper. Coat the balls with edible coloured or glitter dust. Leave to dry out for 2 hours until firm.

5 Make the cream cheese frosting. Beat the butter and icing sugar together until light and fluffy. Add flavourings of choice and beat again. Add the cream cheese and whisk until light and fluffy. Do not over-beat, however, as the mixture can become runny. Place the frosting in a piping bag fitted with a star nozzle and pipe swirls on top of each cupcake. Top each cupcake with the coloured sugarpaste balls and edible metallic balls. Keep for 2 days in an airtight container in a cool place.

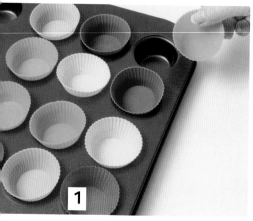
1

2

4

Step-by-Step, Practical Recipes Cupcakes: Tips & Hints

Helpful Hint

Decorating cupcakes can be a great activity for a child's birthday party. Simply bake the cakes slightly in advance, mix up several bowls of different coloured icing, lay out a variety of fun toppings and let each child decorate cupcakes in their own style. They can eat one straight away and take others home with them at the end of the party instead of the traditional slice of birthday cake!

Helpful Hint

Stamps and cutters in almost any imaginable shape can be bought from specialist cake and baking stores. They come in classic metal cookie-cutter styles, in plastic, or as a plunger-style.

Helpful Hint

When it comes to choosing cases to bake your cupcakes in, there is a wealth of choice out there. If it is colourful and patterned cases you are after, it is best to choose from the thicker and greaseproof variety which hold in oil and moisture and remain looking pretty. Silicone cupcake cases are also great as they hold their shape and peel away easily from the sponge. These also come in a variety of shapes including hearts, which can make a cute twist for a special occasion.

Food Fact

According to history, the first cupcakes didn't come with a sweet icing but were instead topped with a savoury gravy-like liquid. The sweet icing we recognise today only became popular and widespread following a wise suggestion by Winston Churchill – little did he know that the product would come to be one today's best-loved baked goods.

Tasty Tip

Once completely cooled, undecorated cupcakes can be frozen for up to three months by wrapping carefully in several layers of cling film or foil and placing within a freezer bag. When you are ready to eat them, defrost the cupcakes at room temperature for several hours; once the sponge is fully defrosted prepare your icing, decorate as normal and enjoy!

Helpful Hint

Measuring dry ingredients when baking is very important – too much or too little of any ingredient can change the end result quite substantially. This applies especially to raising agents like baking powder, bicarbonate of soda and cream of tartar. It is a good idea to invest in a set of measuring spoons.

Helpful Hint

Always try to fill your cupcake cases ½ to ⅔ full of mixture so that when it rises in the oven the finished cupcake is the perfect size to be deliciously substantial whilst still leaving enough room for that all important icing swirl!

Tasty Tip

Cupcakes coated in buttercream can be decorated with colourful sprinkles. To make this easy, place the sprinkles in a small saucer or on a piece of nonstick baking parchment and roll the outside edges of each cupcake in the decorations.

Tasty Tip

For the best possible taste you should eat your cupcakes within 48 hours. You should avoid having to store them in the refrigerator as this will dry the sponge and draw flavour out of the icing. Instead store them in a dry airtight container somewhere cool and away from direct sunlight.

Tasty Tip

When using buttercream and cream cheese frostings, do not be mean with the amount of frosting you use. If this is scraped on thinly, you will see the cake underneath, so be generous. You should also keep cupcakes with frostings in a cool place.

Helpful Hint

Be sure to bring all your ingredients to room temperature before you start adding them to your cupcake mixture. This will help you to avoid a lumpy mixture which would require over-mixing to correct – something which can result in the final cupcake being too chewy in texture. Place a folded tea towel under the mixing bowl if creaming or mixing your cupcake mixture by hand. This stops the bowl slipping around and makes the whole operation quicker and easier.

First published in 2013 by
FLAME TREE PUBLISHING LTD
Crabtree Hall, Crabtree Lane, Fulham,
London, SW6 6TY, United Kingdom
www.flametreepublishing.com

NOTE: Recipes using uncooked eggs should be avoided by infants, the elderly, pregnant women and anyone suffering from an illness.

18 17 16 15 14 13   10 9 8 7 6 5 4 3 2 1

ISBN: 978-0-85775-853-8

ACKNOWLEDGEMENTS: Authors: Ann Nicol, Catherine Atkinson, Juliet Barker, Gina Steer, Vicki Smallwood, Carol Tennant, Mari Mererid Williams, Elizabeth Wolf-Cohen and Simone Wright. Photography: Colin Bowling, Paul Forrester and Stephen Brayne. Home Economists and Stylists: Jacqueline Bellefontaine, Mandy Phipps, Vicki Smallwood and Penny Stephens. Some props supplied by Barbara Stewart at Surfaces. Publisher and Creative Director: Nick Wells. Editorial: Catherine Taylor, Laura Bulbeck, Esme Chapman, Emma Chafer and Karen Fitzpatrick. Design and Production: Chris Herbert, Mike Spender and Helen Wall.